The Native American Indigenous Church Inc.

SomaVeda® Level One

Fundamentals of Thai Yoga Work Book
Indigenous, Traditional Religious Therapeutics: **Native Thai Ayurveda**

One of many traditional asana or postures.
Drawing taken from stone figures located in the courtyard of the Thai Temple, Phraa Wat Chetaphon
Indigenous, Traditional Thai Ayurveda, Indigenous Traditional Thai Massage

Ajahn, Dr. Anthony B. James DNM(P), ND(T), MD(AM).
NAIC Approved Course

Native American Indigenous Church Inc. (NAIC)

SomaVeda® Level One, Fundamentals of Thai Yoga Workbook

Indigenous, Traditional Religious Therapeutics: Native Thai Ayurveda

Publisher: Meta Journal Press

Copyright © 1991-2026 by Anthony B. James DNM(P), ND(T), MD(AM). All rights reserved under International and Pan-American Copyright conventions. World rights reserved. No part of this book may be reproduced or utilized in any form or by any means, electronic or mechanical, including photocopying and recording, or by any information storage and retrieval system, without permission in writing from the publisher. This book contains the proprietary, intellectual property of the SomaVeda Integrated Traditional Therapies® Indigenous, Religious Therapeutics Certification Program.

Inquiries should be addressed to: Anthony B. James C/O NAIC, Inc. 8491 Central Ave. Brooksville, FL 34613 USA (706) 358-8646

ISBN: 978-1-886338-06-7

The Thai Yoga Center: ThaiYogaCenter.Com
Native American Indigenous Church Inc. (NAIC) NativeFireChurch.org
American College of Natural Medicine NAIC-EDU.org
Facebook.Com/LearnThaiYoga

See also: BeardedMedia.com for Uniforms and SomaVeda® Educational Materials
E-Mail: directory@thaiyogacenter.com

This course in its entirety may only be taught by SomaVeda® Certified Facilitators or Instructors in good standing.

_____ #_____

Certified SomaVeda® Instructor and or Facilitators Name and Certificate Number

Thailand

Thailand is in Southeast Asia between 5 degrees north parallel, 21 degrees north parallel, 97 degrees east latitude, and 106 degrees longitude. It is bordered by the countries of Myanmar (Burma), Kampuchea (Cambodia), Laos, and Malaysia.

The terrain is quite diverse, with subtropical lowlands bordered by the Gulf of Siam in the south, the spacious, great central plains of the Menam Chao Phraya, and the craggy mountains of the Northern Highlands. Note that, centrally located in South and Southeast Asia, Thailand is not far from India, China, and the Philippines by land, river, or sea.

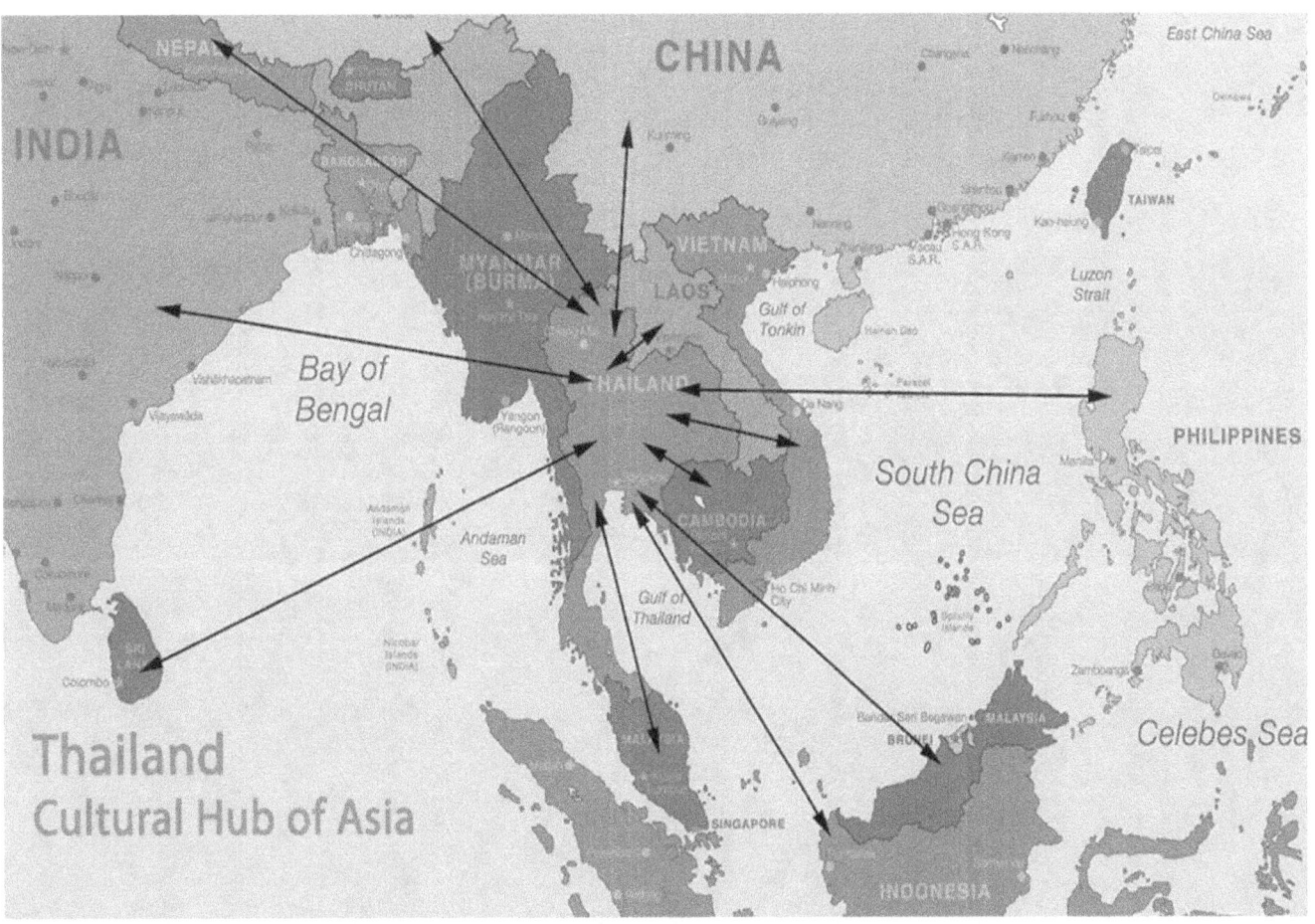

> "Man must himself by his resolute efforts rise and make his way to the portals that give upon liberty and it is always, at every moment in his power so to do. Neither are those portals locked and the key in possession of someone else from whom it must be obtained by prayer and entreaty. That door is free of all bolts and bars save those that man himself has made."

Shakyamuni Buddha
(Piyadassi Thera, Pali translation)

"Ryksaa Thang Nuat Phan Boran Thai," "The Practical expression of loving kindness," is an indigenous, traditional Ayurveda-based healing art. For over 4000 years, the roots of Ayurveda have been documented in practice.

The direct lineage of Thai Ayurveda traces back to Jivaka, or Shivago Komalaboat, who was a personal friend and physician to the Buddha. A student of Atreya and the Medicine Buddha Vaidurya, the Patron Saint of Indian and Tibetan Medicine, is also credited with spreading indigenous, traditional Ayurveda to the Sangha, the Buddhist order of monks and nuns during the Buddha's lifetime. They found the medicine healing and restorative. It relieved many of their aches and pains and enabled them to sit for long hours in deep meditation. Additional influences on traditional medicine came from indigenous peoples of Burma, including the Shan, Mon, Khymer, and Majapaihit/Malay cultures. Thai Ayurveda (ITTM) incorporates all five Ayurvedic disciplines and the Eight Limbs of Yoga/Yoga Therapy. ITTM primarily focuses on the hands-on healing practices of Marma Chikitsa.

The monks and nuns cherished the teachings of Shivago, which came to be known as Traditional Thai Medical Massage, called 'nuat phan boran thai,' which means 'the old Thai way of healing with the hands .'They preserved the teachings, handing them down from one generation to the next in an oral tradition. Each Master, in turn, would personally transmit and pass on the lineage and knowledge to the next generation in the solemn ceremony of the oral tradition. The four principal methods used in traditional healing by the monks are Wai Khruu (Prayers and Spiritual Practice), Herbs (Traditional Medicines), Diet (Sacred nutrition balancing Dosha through food and eating), and Laying On of Hands (Chirothesia or blessing the suffering with healing hands as a spiritual expression). These healing methods require years of intense and disciplined practice.

For a more detailed and thorough description and history of Nuad Boran, see "Ayurveda of Thailand" by Meta Journal Press by the same author.

Ajahn,
Anthony B. James, DNM(P), ND(T), MD(AM)
36th. Generation Instructor, Personal apprentice,
Gold Sash, given the Buddhai Sawan Lineage under
Phaa Khruu, Grand Master Samaii Mesamarn
Grand Master, Certified "Ajahn", Professor of Thai Traditional
Medicine, Winagklaikangwan Industrial College, Hua Hin, Thailand
(Anantasuk School, Wat Po Association),
UTTS registered Lifetime Member # 520121896

Buddhai Sawan Instructor Award Ceremony, Nongkam Thailand 1984

Chief Instructor

1984 marks the year Dr. Anthony B. James became the second non-ethnic Thai initiated into a direct lineage and honored as a Khruu or Teacher. Mr. James was a personal apprentice of the 36th generation Thai Grand Master Phaa Khruu Samaii Mesamarn of The Buddhai Swan Institute. He went on to research, train, gaining recognition in many of the remaining lineages of Thai traditional medicine, including but not limited to:

Vipassana Bhavana & Meditation, Venerable, Aachan Cha

The Traditional College of Medicine under Grand Master Phaa Khruu Men, Aachan Boonsorn Kitnywan (Nuad Phan Boran Thai), Phrakhru Uppakarn Phatanakit, Khruu Moh Vilapong Sidtisapong • 02/16/91 The Provincial Hospital in Chiang Mai under Master Phaa Khruu, Aachan, Sintorn Chaichagun, Institute Training Massage (ITM- Chiangmai) Aachan John Chongkol

Jap Sen- Tok Sen Nuat with "Mama" Lek Chaiya Sawankhalok Syle Blind Massage under Aachan Tawee Anantasuk Nuad and Thai Korosot under Phaa Khruu Anantasuk

Anantasuk Nuad and Nuad Prakhop Samun Prai, Aachan Nanntipa Anantasuk Vajrayana Tibetan Buddhism under Yeshe Lobsang Tinsen Negi of Tibet and Darmsala.

The modern expression of this ancient healing discipline has been translated and creatively adapted to the needs of the modern West by Ajahn James. Authorized Tribal Health Care Provider (NAIC), Traditional Naturopath (ANMA), and founder of the Native American Indigenous Church (NAIC) specializing in Spiritually based, Indigenous, and Traditional Holistic and Natural Alternative or Complementary Medicine.

Ajahn, Dr. James, authored the very first Thai Traditional Massage book ever published in English in 1981. First used as a manuscript in class for the first three years, it was formally published in 1984 after being given teacher certification and recognition. It was used exclusively to teach privately in class until 1984, when it was released to the public and distributed worldwide, beginning a tidal wave of interest that continues today. This first influential book, and still one of the most often sourced and quoted books on Thai Yoga, is titled "Nuat Thai, Traditional Thai Medical Massage". The newest edition is available at BeardedMedia.Com ("Ayurveda of Thailand: Indigenous Traditional Thai Medicine and Thai Yoga Therapy" Meta Journal Press https://beardedmedia.com/product/ayurveda-of-thailand-book/).

Dr. James is the founder and the system's original certified instructor. He has devoted more than 35 years to the creation and development of SomaVeda® Thai Yoga as an effective form of Ayurveda, Yoga Therapy, and Natural Medicine. This work has been formally recognized by the Royal Government of Thailand and current regulatory bodies: awarded the prestigious "Friend of Thailand Award" in 2002, Ajahn and Master Teacher in 2006, and Lifetime Teacher Status with The Union Of Thai Traditional Medicine Society in 2010.

Benefits:

Thai Yoga Therapy facilitates and promotes a harmonious state of being. The ancient Thai carefully recorded various states of disease and imbalances in the body, mind, and emotions, and, over time, devised methods to influence their course. Promoting a harmonious state of being is essential, as these imbalances often keep people from experiencing life fully and productively. If a person suffered injury or trauma, Nuad or Thai Yoga was the primary vehicle for rehabilitation. Thai Yoga is an excellent alternative therapy for rehabilitation, pain relief, and stress reduction. It is nurturing, calming, and enlivening, and will expand ideas about bodywork.

Outcomes: The direct result of a SomaVeda® Thai Yoga therapy session is called PROMIIWIHAN SII or the Four Boundless States of Mind. These are Boundless Love, Boundless Compassion, Boundless Joy, and Boundless Equanimity. All other results are secondary or less valuable.

SomaVeda® Thai Yoga Therapy: There are over 100 clinical benefits to Somaveda® Thai Yoga documented!

1. Enhances the body/mind connection
2. Reduces Stress and enhances the sense of well being Relaxes and Loosens tight muscles
3. Reduces pain
4. Reduces swelling and edema, Increases range of motion
5. Effective in Psycho-Somatic and Psychological illness. Helps many kinds of Soft tissue-related disorders. Assists in stress-related Infertility and Impotence, Reduces Chronic Fatigue and Related Syndromes
6. Facilitates Lymphatic Drainage and supports proper immune system response
7. Reduces Karmic Blockage and Stagnation

SomaVeda® Thai Yoga, a system of Traditional and Indigenous Traditional Medicine and Chirothesia, incorporates mindfulness, gentle rocking, deep stretching, and rhythmic compression to create a singular healing experience. This work, a unique form of Vajrayana Yoga, developed initially in schools of Indigenous, Traditional Thai Ayurveda (ITTM) and Vipassana Meditation, focuses on balancing energy and creating wholeness of mind, body, and spirit in the client and the practitioner.

SomaVeda® is generally received fully clothed, unlike many Western forms of massage or bodywork. Proper attire consists of an approved school uniform, a School logo T-shirt, or a top made of loose-fitting, comfortable, natural-fiber clothing, preferably cotton. Avoid tight or restrictive clothing such as jeans. Think of clothing suitable for relaxing and stretching in a gentle yoga-like manner.

Please note: For female participants, there is a better time to focus on support. Tight or underwire bras can be detrimental to energy/physiology and potentially a painful distraction as we move from position to position. Men should avoid heavy belts and buckles. All jewelry should be removed and placed away before practice begins.

SomaVeda® uses the whole person to treat the whole person.

The Native American Indigenous Church, Inc.
SomaVeda® Level One

General Method Puja

> " He who would have the better of the end should strive to have the better of the beginning" Michael Montaigne

Five Phases or Steps:

Sit comfortably next to the client. Sit on the **Left Side** for a **woman** and on the **Right Side** for a **man**. This practice acknowledges the natural polarity of the client and follows a traditional form of practice. If you can't discern sex, go with what the client gives you!

1. **Acknowledge The Space:** Visualize the Energetic or Matrix body at fifty feet, then becoming denser at about six feet. Understand that if any space shared is holy or sacred, it must be so for this space.

2. **Seek Refuge (Wai Khruu):** Acknowledge the lineage. We have a lineage. What is it? In their Wai Khruu, the Thai say OM NAMO SHIVAGO, paying respect to three Buddhas - Great Buddha, Boddhisatva, Inner Buddha, or Conscience Teacher. Before touching, know who you-the the therapist's role is in this encounter, why the therapist is here, and from where the healing energy or connection comes. Love manifests through the connection and the hands now.

3. **Clean House:** Ask, "Is there anything that keeps me from being with this person beside me in the best possible healing way now?" There are only two possible answers: If the answer is no, then continue. If the answer is yes, it will fall into one of two categories:
1) Issues that can be handled now, and
2) 2) Issues that cannot be handled now and must be postponed. If there is a decision to postpone an issue, the therapist MUST address it when able.

4. **Petition and Prayer:** Sometimes, all we need is ONE PERSON to agree with us for our healing to manifest. Generate the Bodhicitta, perfect mind, perfect thought. May all living beings be happy and free from suffering. May all living beings reach enlightenment and no longer be subject to the cycle of birth, death, and rebirth. For the client: May this person receive all the healing and resolution of their difficulty that they can now receive. May all the beneficial and healing energies, inclined and able to move through the therapist to help this person, do so NOW.

NAIC, Inc.

SomaVeda® Level One

General Method: Puja Continued

5. Listening and Connecting:

Continue by being patient and acknowledging the state of the client before proceeding. An acknowledgment will provide a baseline to gauge changes in the client as the sessions progress. There are many different rhythms of life, and everything that lives and moves carries a record of this movement in its unique pulse.

We begin with three primary pulses: Breath, Cardiopulmonary, and Peristalsis. These are gross, physical, and pervasive rhythms. Learn to see the obvious before looking for the subtle.

THE BREATH:
1) Are They Breathing?
2) Where is the breath? The breath is always somewhere
3) Where is the breath going? The breath is always going somewhere.

THE HEART
1) Is the Heart beating?
2) Describe several qualities of the heartbeat. Is it fast? Slow? Regular?

THE DIGESTION
1) Moving? Which direction?

Puja is just a part of a more extensive practice called "Wai Khruu." Wai Khruu is the medicine appropriate for Karmic and spiritually based diseases. The Term means to pay respect to three Buddhas or teachers. Who are the three teachers? 1) Jesus the Christ, Creator Sets Free, Great Buddha, God, Great Spirit, Innate whoever or whatever is the ultimate original or absolute consciousness or creator. 2) Boddhisatva's, or Flesh and blood persons who help our progress. 3) Inner Buddha, inner teacher, or conscience. The innate part of us knows what is right.

Note: The hollow tube visualization may be helpful for Puja.

NAIC, Inc.

SomaVeda® Level One

The Warm Up

1) Palm Walk out and back on the Feet.

Begin in a seated position, positioned well below the feet. (Palm walking means to alternate hand pressure just like you would in normal walking)

2) Palm Walk up the lower leg.

The fingers of both hands are kept close together and always point upward toward the stomach, except when holding the Wind Gates (Lom) at the top of the legs. At these points, the fingers are pointing AWAY from the center line.

3) Palm Circles on the Knees.

4) Palm Walk up, Open the Wind, Palm Walk down the upper leg.

5) Palm circles on the knees

6) Palm Walk the feet.

Proceed up the legs, and take steps as long as the length of the hands, from the finger tip to the heel of the hand. Drop the shoulders. Keep the arms straight. The hands should be very relaxed with no hard edges. Sway the body from side to side as the hands are shifted from point to point. On the feet, the

Big Reminder: Look THROUGH the hands NOT AT THEM!

NOTE:
The warm-up is relaxing and suitable preparation for the body of the session. It grounds, centers, and balances chakras #1 & #4. It draws the Prana, or Chi, lower into the abdomen and reduces internal antagonistic tension, making the client more pliable and generally receptive to our beneficial energy.

Supine Position

Puja Warm Up

(1) Supine Lateral Leg

Stretch and Palm Press 3X

(2) Supine Foot Routine (*Lang Tao*)

3 lines 1X, Circle & Pull Toes

(3) Supine Posterior Upper Leg (*Ya Na Ka*)

Push the leg, Foot Press 3x

(4) Open the Wind (*Bput Bpa Tu Lom*)

Palm Press, Hold for ten count

(5) Supine Anterior Arm (Two Positions)

Press Shoulder 10 count, Palm Press medial arm 3X, Stretch and Palm Press lateral arm 3X

(1-5) Repeat # 1-5--

NAIC, Inc.

SomaVeda® Level One

Supine Position

Supine lateral Leg :

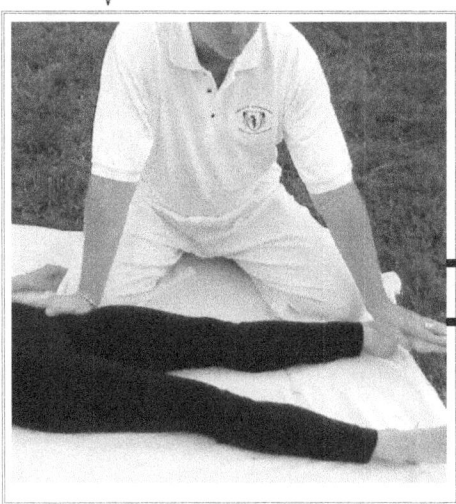

Stretch and Palm Press 3X.

Frame your work area with the Knees.

Top Hand Travels
(top is closest to the client's head).

Supine Anterior Foot Routine (*Lang Tao*):
Straighten the Leg

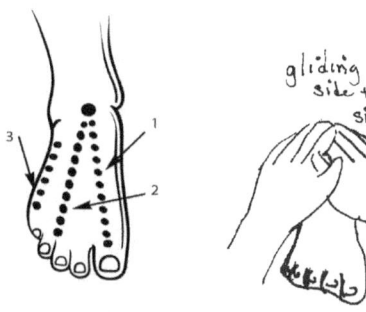

Work 3 Line 3X with Snake Thumb

On line #3 (Outside line), use "pinch and drag."

Circle and Pull the Toes

Supine Posterior Upper Leg (*Ya Na Ka*):

Push the Leg 3X

Use the <u>inside</u> foot as the working tool.

Push primarily with the heel of the foot.

Support the client's bent leg on your <u>outside leg</u>.

Hold both ankles with your hands.

Come out smoothly, being careful to fully

support their knee as you transition to the next

technique.

NAIC, Inc.

SomaVeda® Level One

Supine Position

Open The Wind
(*Bput bpa tu lom*):

Reinforced Palm Press and Hold for 10 Count.
1. Determine the borders of Femoral Triangle
2. Mark the Pulse location.
3. Cover the Pulse. Fingers pointing away from the center.
4. Shift weight to press. WAM* moves toward its center line.
5. Pause before leaving, feel the heat.

* WAM: Weight Activation Mechanism (Your hips and bottom!)

Stay below the Inguinal Line, medial to Sartorius and lateral to Gracilis muscles.

Supine Arm (Two Positions):

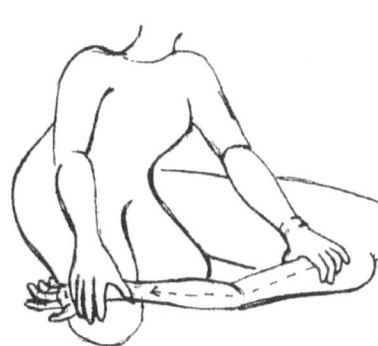

Hold Shoulder Point (Lom) (Feel the heat) Palm Press medial arm 3X. (Inside hand) Stretch & Palm Press lateral arm 3X.
(Top hand travels)

> **Frame the Work Area**
> **Keep the Head Up**
> **Look Through the Arms and Hands, Keep the Back Straight**
> **Keep the Arms Straight Rock and Breathe to Create Pressure**

NAIC, Inc.
SomaVeda® Level One
Fundamentals of Thai Yoga

THE FLOWING PRACTICE

Definition of FLOW: Flow is when you emphasize the transitions and spaces between techniques as much or more than the techniques themselves.

Simply put, FLOW MEANS GO! Set up and acknowledge each step as if going to execute it; however, do not. Instead, ACKNOWLEDGE the position or technique, then continue. It only takes as long as a snap of the fingers to make an acknowledgment. During flowing practice, draw the lines with light pressure rather than pressing with working pressure. Pause briefly at the points one typically holds or circles, then continue.

An excellent flowing attitude is smooth, seamless, slow, continuous, superficial, and mindful. Flow practice is the best way to practice SomaVeda® Thai, as it takes about 30 flowing sessions to get to the first practice hallmark of competency.

More about Thai Yoga

Traditional Thai medical theory is unique. It is a form and practice of traditional, classical Ayurveda influenced by regional practices and culture. It is a derivative of Tibetan, Indian, and Chinese Medicine, nurtured and cultivated by Thai Buddhist Monks. It reflects the country's diversity and blend of ethnicities, such as large Chinese, Hindu, Tribal, and Muslim populations. It is essentially a Yogic system based upon the theory of Chakras and Sen or Prana Nadis. However, with a thousand years of Chinese influence, the Thais have no problem relating to meridians and acupuncture points.

The practitioner of medicine has several different categories of specialization, including but not limited to Marma-Chikitsa & Bone setting, Yoga/ Ayurveda, Prayers & Meditation, Acupuncture/ Bloodletting, Moxibustion & Medicinal Incense, Herbal Pharmacology & Medicines, Herbal and Oil Massage, Herbal Steam & Medicinal Baths, Hot and Cold Therapies, Dietary Therapies, Purging Therapies, i.e., Enemas, Purgatives, and Emetics (Pancha Karma). Also included are natural therapies and substances derived from nature, such as Air (Lom), fire/light (Fai), earth (Din), and water (Nam), which are in almost endless combinations.

Any therapeutic discipline developed over thousands of years, serving millions of souls, is bound to have depth and diversity! It takes seven to fifteen years to master any major treatment category. However, a good doctor will have mastered several and have a working knowledge of all the rest. Hence, in Thailand, there are "Marma Chikitsa" doctors (Maw Nuad) who know herbs, or possibly "Herbal Doctors" who offer Thai Nuad-Marma Chikitsa or acupuncture/acupressure.

Supine Position Notes:

Side Lying Position, (S.L.P)

(1) Inferior Leg (Leg closest to the floor)
Stretch & Palm Press 3X

(2) Inferior Foot & Stretch
Elbow Press, Rotate Ankle & Press foot to the bottom

(3) Superior Leg (Leg closest to the ceiling)
Palm Press 3X

(4) Lower/Middle Lamina Groove (Above the spine)
Thumb Press 3X

(5) Upper Lamina Groove (Lateral Cervical)
Thumb Press 3X

(6) Spinal Rotation and Stretch

(1-6)---

NAIC, Inc.

SomaVeda® Level One

Side Lying Position

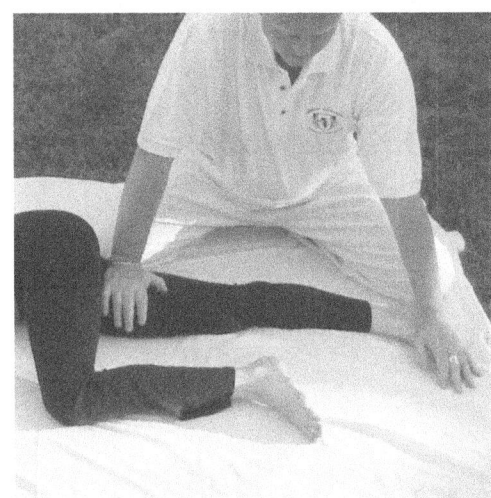

S.L.P. Inferior leg :

**Stretch and Palm Press 3X
Top hand travels, bottom hand is stationary Points are one palm width apart**

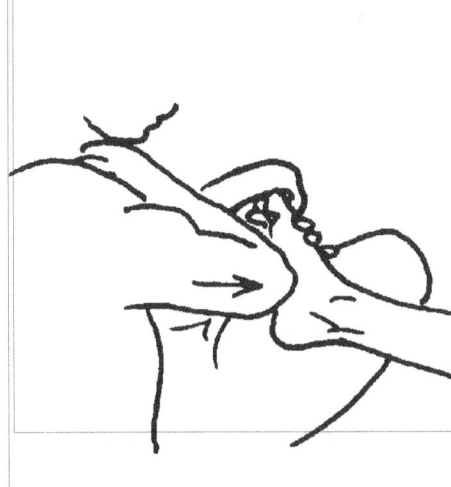

S.L.P. Inferior Foot & Stretch:
Elbow Press Foot 1X

Top knee goes behind their knee. Prop their foot up on your lower legs upper thigh and lean all the way forward to create pressure. Move their foot to change points.

Rotate Ankle 5X each way
Stretch foot to bottom and hold for 5 count

Fold their leg over to press heel toward bottom do not change your position.

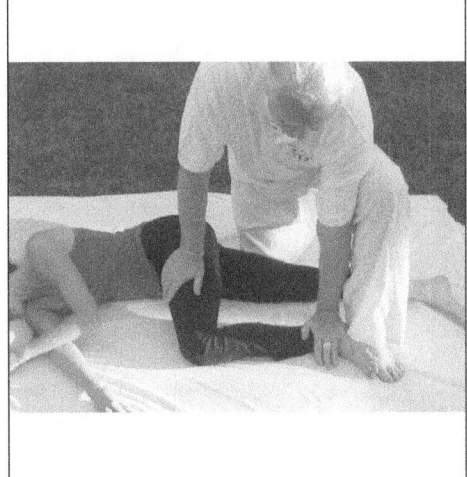

S.L.P. Superior Leg:

Palm Press 3X
Step over into lunge position first, then rock forward to create pressure. Breath! Sink!
Top Hand Travels (down-up-down).

S.L.P. Lower / Middle Lamina Groove :

Reinforced Rolling Thumb 3X. Frame work area between wide knees Sit up straight
Rock and Breath to create pressure. Work points one thumb length apart

S.L.P. Upper Lamina & Lateral Cervical:

Thumb Press side of neck 3X.
Step over the head into lunge position. Work points 1 thumb width apart.

S.L.P. Spinal Rotation & Stretch:

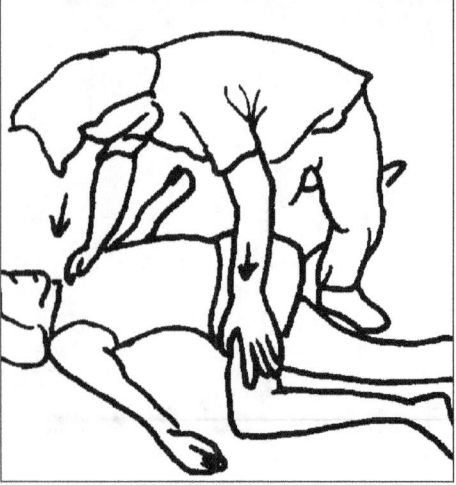

Position your spine at right angles to the axis of rotation. Both knees are down. One hand on the shoulder and one below the knee. Press slowly with the breath.

We do not do specific adjustments. We do Passive, Assisted, Non-Ballistic, Facilitated, Range of Motions only.

NAIC, Inc.
SomaVeda® Level One
Note

Body Mechanics and Angle of Attack:

The higher the point or line being worked, the higher the center of gravity should be relative to the specific body parts and the floor. The lower or more acute the angle of the point is,
relative to the body part and floor, the lower the working center of gravity.

Simply stated, If the lines are on top, so are you! Go high. If the line is on the side, so are you! Go low!

THERE ARE NO MISTAKES IN SomaVeda® Thai Yoga...
ONLY
FURTHER REFINEMENTS!

Prone Position

(1)   Palming The Back

Bi-Lateral Palm Press up and down 1X

(2)   Cross Stretching The Back

Palm Walk with Rotation up and down each side 1X

(3)   Walk on The Legs

Stand and walk 3X, Walk on Feet

(4)   Prone Torso & Gluteal Points

Kneel on glutes, Palm Walk Back 3X

(5)   The Cobra

Pull up 1X

NAIC, Inc.
SomaVeda® Level One
Prone Position

Palming The Back:

Bi-Lateral Palm Press up and down: 1X.

Step across the torso into the lunge position to work.

The fingers of both hands are pointing away from the spine.

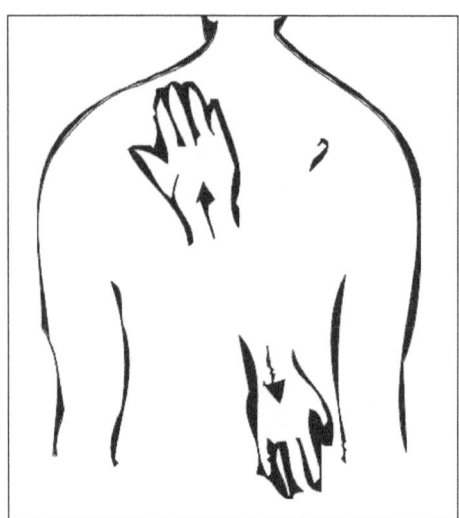

Cross Stretching The Back:

Palm Walk with Rotation up and down each side 1X. Imagine a line between the opposite fingers at all times

Start with the hands close and fingers pointing away or outward. The walk down one side only, while turning the fingers away from each other. However, keeping the fingers always on the same line between them.

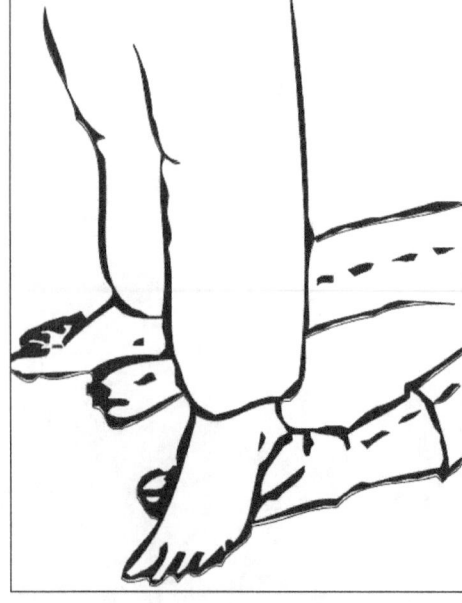

Walk on the Legs:

Stand and walk on the legs and the feet: 3X.

Walk on the upper leg first. (round arch to round bottom,) then the lower leg. Do both legs before going to the feet.

Walk on the feet.

First walk with the balls of the feet, then heels. Be delicate and thoughtful when placing your weight on their feet.

NAIC, Inc.

SomaVeda® Level One

Prone Position: Prone Torso & Gluteal Points:

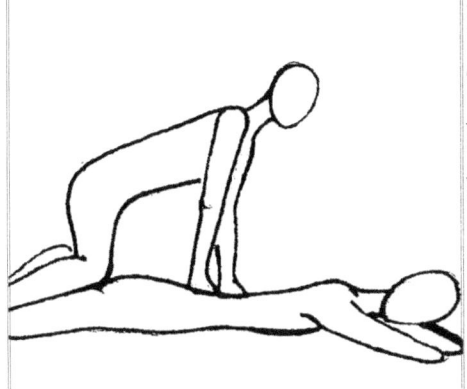

Kneel on glutes, Palm Walk Back 3X

To accommodate your weight for your client, simply shift your bottom forward to become heavier and shift backward to become lighter. Think light, be light.

The Cobra:

Pull the client upward gently. "Hold my arms."

Relax your shoulders.

Sit low and lean back into a back bend. Return to mat slowly.

Relax
Frame the Work Area
Keep theHead Up
Look Through the Arms and
Hands Keep the Back Straight
Keep the Arms

NAIC, Inc.
SomaVeda® Level One
Prone Position Notes:

NAIC, Inc.

SomaVeda® Level One

Notes

BE GENTLE TO YOURSELF:

Minor stiffness, soreness, or difficulty moving is likely to be noticed. A small amount of stiffness and soreness is predictable and okay. In this training, you use your body in ways that may be unfamiliar—kneeling and moving about on the floor,
bending and stretching, especially the wrist and ankles. Body parts not heard from in a while, maybe updating on the new stress. Do not be alarmed. This practice has a training and conditioning effect, as expected from any new fitness or Yoga practice.

As you continue to practice, your level of conditioning will adapt, and the soreness will dissipate.

> To help in this regard, move slowly and deliberately while in class. Avoid fast or hurried movements. While moving about on the floor, be gentle and walk softly on the knees. Make no bouncing or banging sounds while moving. Use the whole palm of your hand to help move around. Using the whole hand to support helps distribute weight over more of the body, reducing stress on any particular part. It is appropriate to let your instructor know if you are incredibly sore. They will likely be able to help you.

> We say, "SomaVeda® is as much for the person doing it as it is for the lucky one receiving." While advancing in this practice, you will learn how to maximize all Asanas or Postures for the best advantage of yourself and your client. Examples would be stepping deeper into the lunge or leaning farther into a bend, breathing more deeply, cultivating Puja and the meditative mind, reaching for and feeling the essence of the energy at every moment, and cultivating continuity of consciousness and intent from the first moment of the therapeutic encounter to the last.

Second Supine Position (*Sadung*)

(1) Abdominal Circles

Clockwise Palm Circles 30X

(2) Supine Cross Leg Stretch

Cross leg, Pin knee, Support knee and Shoulder, Rotate 1X

(3) Supported Shoulder Stand

Hands on knees, 3 part lift to balance point 1X

(4) Cross Leg Pull Up

Cross ankles below knees, Hold arms & lean back 3X

NAIC, Inc.
SomaVeda® Level One

Second Supine Position

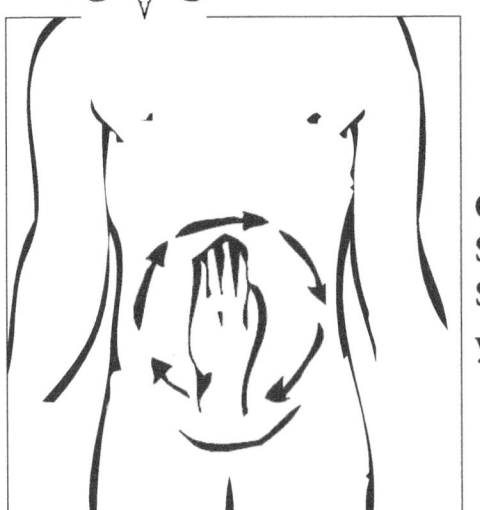

Abdominal Circles:

Clockwise Palm Circles 30X.
Sit perpendicular to the client w/ knees wide.
Sit up straight, breathe, and lean forward and back to you're your hands. Visualize pressure moving into the earth.

Supine Cross Leg Stretch:

[See Spinal Rotation & Stretch]

Brace the superior knee with the lower hand.

Hold the proximal shoulder with the upper hand. Center your body to be perpendicular to the client before pressing.

Push and rotate the knee to the mat on the opposite side.

Move with the breath, stop when the breath runs out, or the knee hits the floor, whichever comes first.

Observe contra-indications.

Release and repeat on the opposite side.

Supported Shoulder Stand:

Hands on knees. 3-part lift to balance point: 1X.

Pull, Turn, and Push to the balance point... No further!

Align your body in such a way that you are stronger at the end of the lift than at the beginning. Squat deeply to lift.

Avoid leaning as much as possible. Look for the point of zero balance. Look for the upside-down triangle. Stay close. Use your inside hip and hand to provide lateral stability.

NAIC, Inc.

SomaVeda® Level One

Second Supine Position

Cross Leg Pull Up:

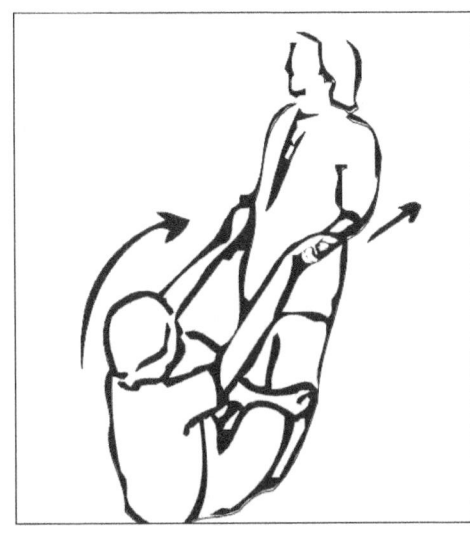

Bump and bend the knees to drop them downward. Cross the ankles below your knees.

Say "Hold my," then hold on to the forearms. Lift with the legs, then lean back.

Drop the shoulders and keep the arms straight. Pull up 3X. Third time, pull into seated position.

Bailout: In SomaVeda®

In SomaVeda®, there are two types of bailouts. The therapists can bail out, or the client can bail out.

A bailout is an attempt to escape, redirect, or mediate the intention that the therapist is trying to facilitate through postural changes. Asanas are direct and specific, and there are predictable points at which individuals may experience distress and try to compensate by readjusting or escaping the pressure. We know this and practice compensatory mechanisms to keep the client in the therapeutic groove.

It is best to work with light pressure and specific focus when working through blockages rather than letting the client's focus wander.

The client may need to be made aware that the therapist is facilitating them into the optimum posture for their release. Recovery also means that if the therapists lapse or momentarily lose control or focus, they can easily reorganize and continue with minimal loss of time, effort, and energy.

NAIC, Inc.
SomaVeda® Level One
Notes
CONTINUOUS BREATHING:

Continuous Breathing is our way of ensuring an unrestricted flow of prana in both participants during the session. It is a simple concept that is easy to master with a bit of practice. On each exertion, push or puff out a little air. A principle states that you can hold your breath until you pop. However, the air will always find its way back in if you blow it out!

Technically, the entire session experience is about facilitating the free and unrestricted flow of Prana, or Chi, both of which translate into English language as vitality/ vital "air or breath."

The breath or breathing pattern of the therapist is always reflected in the client through modeling. If your Breathing is shallow or you are holding your breath, you can be sure your client is breathing similarly.

If you notice that your client is not breathing correctly, before you do

Anything, check your breath before giving advice or coaching the client.

HELP YOUR PARTNER:
When paired up and practicing flow, the receiver's job is to help the partner keep moving. Avoid stopping them by asking questions. Do not tell them to stop and return to a forgotten step. If the partner is flowing and overlooks a technique, make a mental note and review it at the end. There are no mistakes, only lapses while flowing.

Flow means go! It enables us to develop a way of seeing entire sessions as a single therapeutic application of healing presence and intent, rather than a string of unrelated techniques performed in a particular sequence.

Seated Position

(1) **Seated Position Palm Press**

On the shoulders 1,2,3,2,1

(2) **Soft Spinal Rotation**

Both sides

(3) **The 1/2 Whale (Sitting)**

Sit behind or use a bolster to back bend

(4) **Full Forward Bend**

Clients' Feet together, back straight, stand behind and gently push 3X

NAIC, Inc.
SomaVeda® Level One
Seated Position

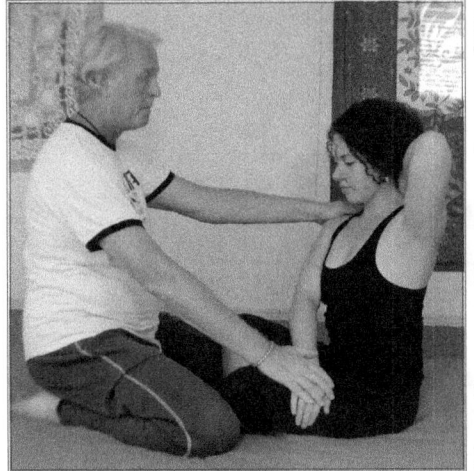

Seated Position Palm Press:

Stand behind the client and

press down onto the top of the shoulders by leaning. The rule is "Perch not Press."

It is a sinking motion, more than a pressing. Follow the breath. 1, 2, 3, 2, 1

Seated Position Soft Spinal Rotation:

While kneeling in front of the client, sit and frame the closest knee, t h e n pull the wrist while pushing the opposite shoulder.

Change sides and repeat the opposite side from the second knee position.

Some beautiful progressions and variations are available from here once you're more comfortable and sensitive to what the client can do.

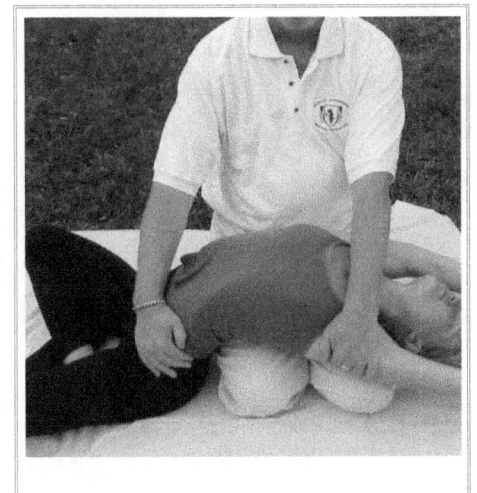

The Whale (Sitting): *Artis Matsyandra*

Sit behind and perpendicular to the client.

Lean them back over your legs as a support for their back bend. Support the head firmly as you do so. When in position, rock them gently to facilitate release. An acceptable alternative is to place a bolster or pillow directly behind you, instead of using your thighs, and continue as before. To release, tuck the chin to the chest, then raise the whole body in one smooth movement.

NAIC, Inc.

SomaVeda® Level One

Seated Position

Seated Position Full Forward Bend:

Paschimottanasana

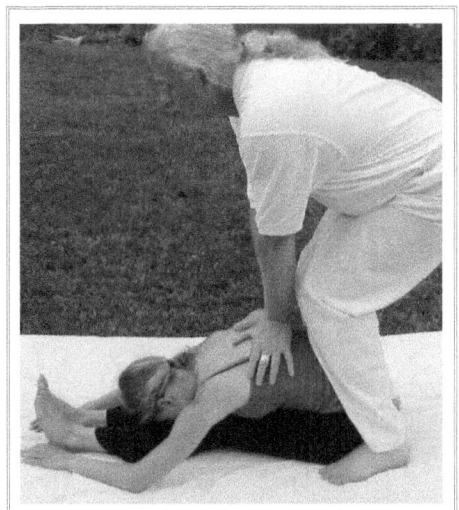

Begin kneeling behind the client.

Coach their legs together and out straight before them.

Sit them up, erect, and breathe in before leaning forward.

Stand then press equally with the shins and knees.

While pressing down between the shoulders with the palms. Follow the breath down 3X. (Each exhale, go a little further) Release and bring up, back over, returning to the supine position in one smooth motion.

Return to the feet of the client Final Warm-up

Return to the appropriate side of the client Puja / Finish

We have completed a great circle and find ourselves at the same point at the end, beginning, and ending with Puja. Remember what Phaa Khruu said," All of the healing which is to take place may do so in Puja. Everything we do may be nothing more than window dressing, something to keep us occupied while the actual healing work occurs."

Be thoughtful and share the newly acquired insight soon, so you don't lose it or diminish its reality. You have now been given and have received a private transmission of this healing lineage by an authentic teacher.

To own this teaching, all that is required is to lay your hands on as many people as possible. As a result of this, you are authorized and empowered by this teacher and all the powers and authority which support this line of healing tradition in the world of Samsara or suffering to share this good way with all whom you meet.

OM NAMO SHIVAGO

NAIC, Inc.
SomaVeda® Level One
Seated Position Notes:

Level One Short General Session

Puja
Warm-up

(A)　　　　　　　　　　Supine Position
  (1)　　　　　　　　　　Supine Lateral Leg
  (2)　　　　　　　　　　Supine Anterior Foot Routine (Lang Tao)
  (3)　　　　　　　　　　Supine Posterior Upper Leg (Ya Na Ka)
  (4)　　　　　　　　　　Open the Wind (Bput Bpa Tu Lom)
  (5)　　　　　　　　　　Supine Anterior Arm
(1-5)--
(B)　　　　　　　　　　Side Lying Position
  (1)　　　　　　　　　　SLP Inferior Leg
  (2)　　　　　　　　　　SLP Inferior foot & Stretch
  (3)　　　　　　　　　　SLP Superior Leg
  (4)　　　　　　　　　　SLP Lower / Middle Lamina Groove
  (5)　　　　　　　　　　SLP Upper Lamina & Lateral Cervical
  (6)　　　　　　　　　　SLP Spinal Rotation and Stretch
(1-6)--
(C)　　　　　　　　　　Prone Position
  (1)　　　　　　　　　　Palming The Back
  (2)　　　　　　　　　　Stretching The Back
  (3)　　　　　　　　　　Walk on The Legs
  (4)　　　　　　　　　　Prone Torso & Gluteal Points
  (5)　　　　　　　　　　The Cobra

(D)　　　　　　　　　　Second Supine Position (Sadung)
  (1)　　　　　　　　　　Abdominal Circles
  (2)　　　　　　　　　　Supine Cross Leg Stretch
(2)--
  (3)　　　　　　　　　　Supported Shoulder Stand
  (4)　　　　　　　　　　Cross Leg Pull Up

(E)　　　　　　　　　　Seated Position
  (1)　　　　　　　　　　Palm Press
  (2)　　　　　　　　　　Soft Spinal Rotation
  (3)　　　　　　　　　　The 1/2 Whale
  (4)　　　　　　　　　　Forward Bend Warm-up

Puja

NAIC, Inc.
SomaVeda® Level One
Notes

Generating The Boddhichitta

The Bodhichita is an example of the most perfect thinking a person can do. It is a perfect petition for the well being of all sentient beings. As a Mantra, it powerfully manifests the loving and compassionate energies of all of the Saints and Sages, and as such, is suitable for inclusion in your Puja.

METTA SUTRA

This is what should be accomplished by the one who is wise, who seeks the good and has obtained peace:

Let one be strenuous, upright, and sincere, without pride, easily contented and joyous;
Let one not be submerged by the things of the world. Let one not take upon oneself the burden of riches; Let one's senses be controlled;
Let one be wise but not puffed up;
Let one not desire great possessions even for one's family;
Let one do nothing that is mean or that the wise would reprove.

May all beings be happy.
May they be joyous and live in safety.
All living beings, whether weak or strong, in high or middle or low realms of existence, small or great, visible or invisible, near or far, born or to be born, may all beings be happy.

Let no one deceive another, nor despise any being in any state; Let none by anger or hatred wish harm to another.

Even as a mother at the risk of her life watches over and protects her only child, so with a boundless mind should one cherish all living things, suffusing love over the entire world, above, below, and all around without limit; So let one cultivate an infinite goodwill toward the whole world.

Standing or walking, sitting or lying down, during all one's waking hours, let one cherish the thought that this way of living is the best in the world.

Abandoning vain discussion, having a clear vision, freed from sense appetites, one who is made perfect will never again know rebirth in the cycle of creation of suffering for ourselves or for others.

32.

SomaVeda®
INDIGENOUS, TRADITIONAL THAI YOGA AYURVEDA

Fundamentals of Thai Yoga/ Thai Massage SomaVeda® Level One Complete Photo Index

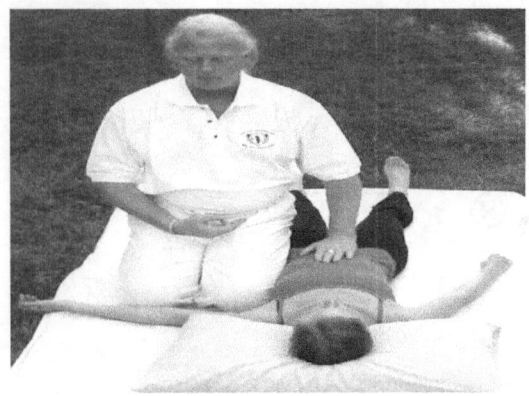
PUJA

Finnish back at Feet

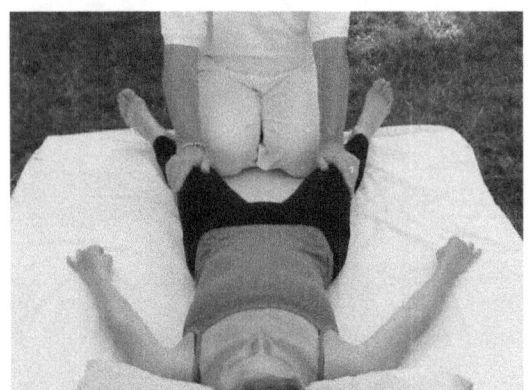
Warm-up the feet

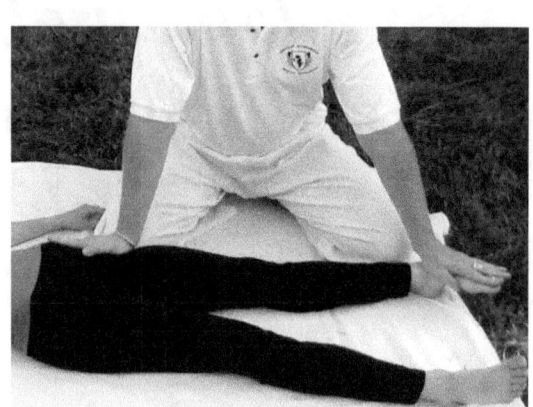
Supine Lateral Leg

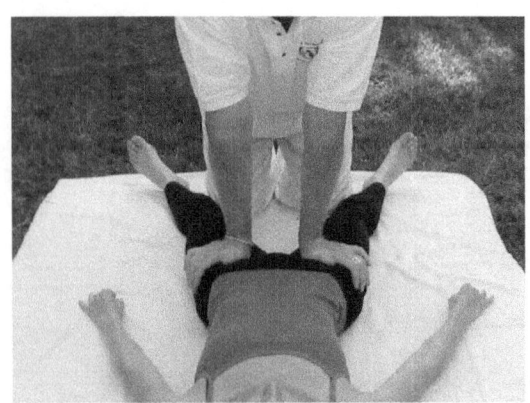
Palm Circles on Knees

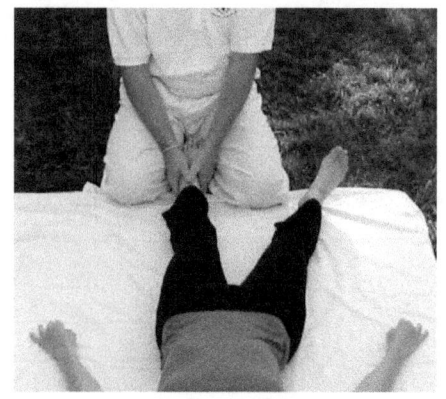
Foot Routine

Open The Wind

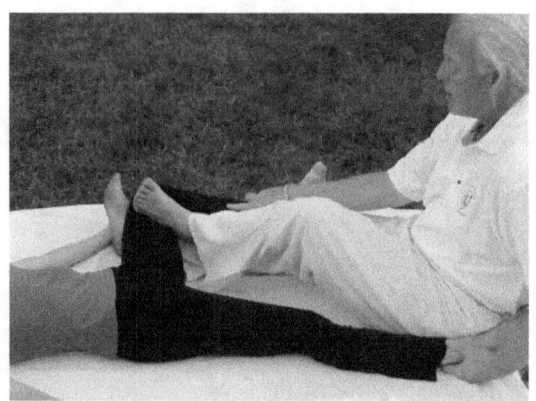
YaNaKa Push the leg)

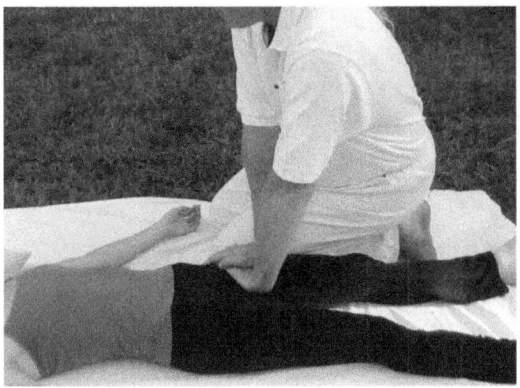

Open The Wind

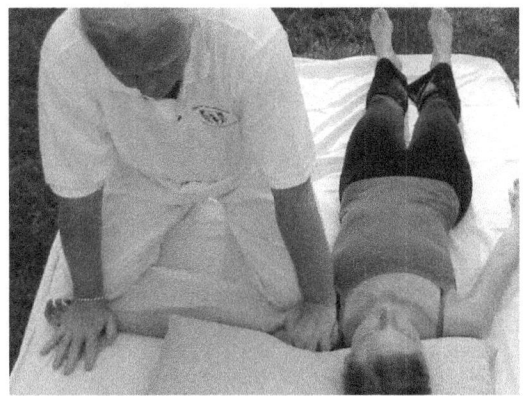

Medial Arm

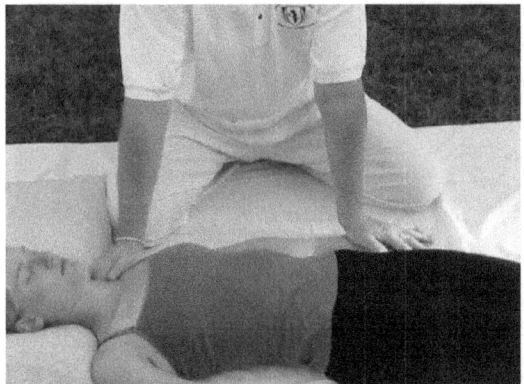

PP Lateral Arm

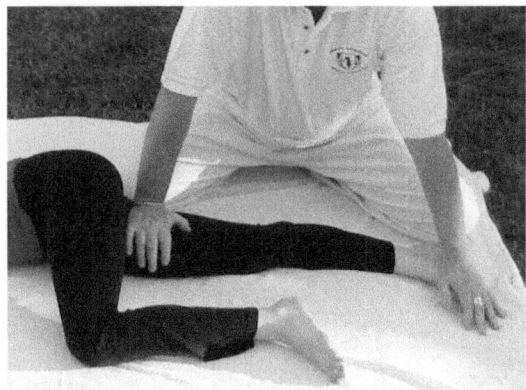

PP Inferior Leg

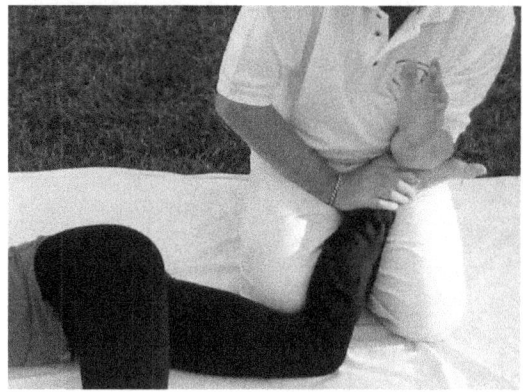

Elbow The Foot

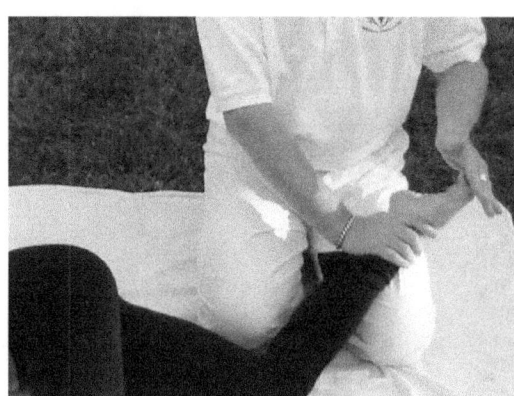

Rotate The Ankle

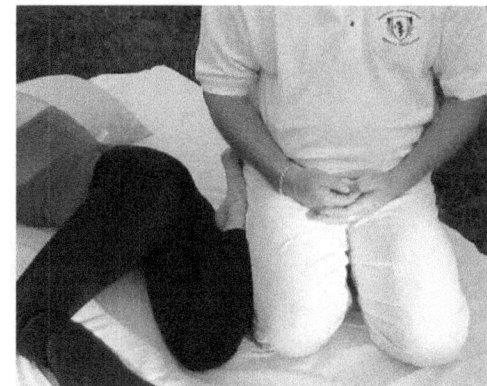

Stretch The Leg

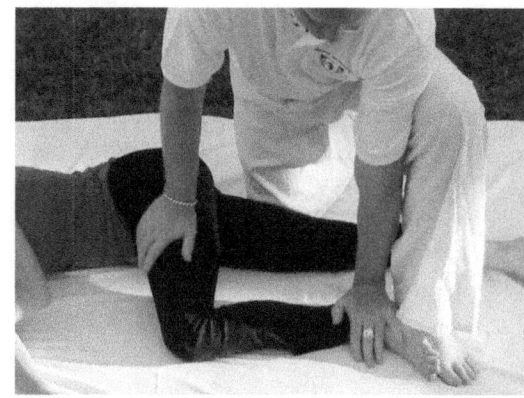

PP Superior Leg

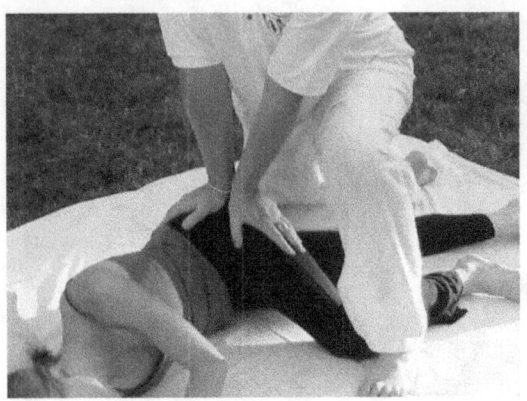
Press The Hip

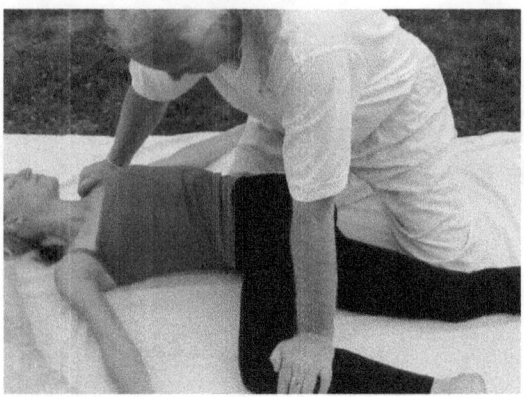
SLP Spinal Rotation

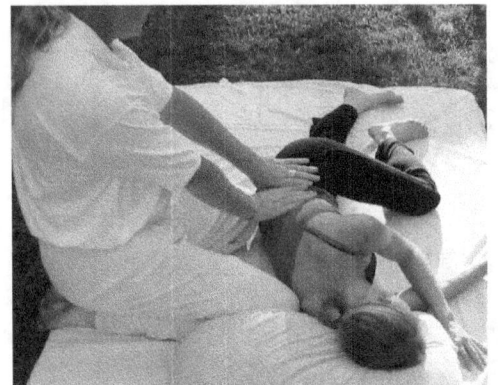
Thumb Press The Back

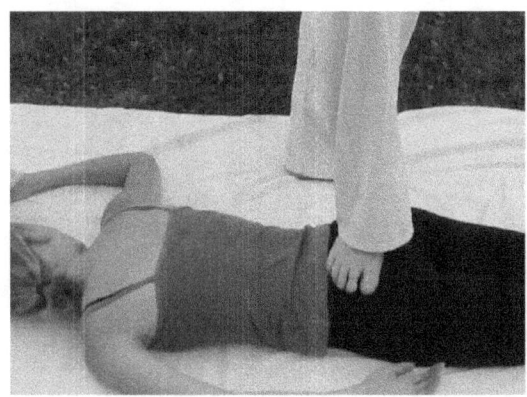
Foot Rocking

Thumb Press The Neck

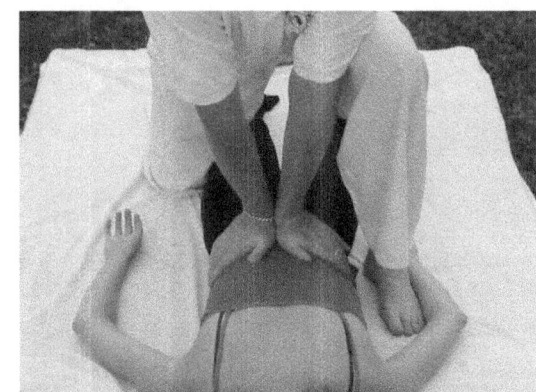
Palm Press Back

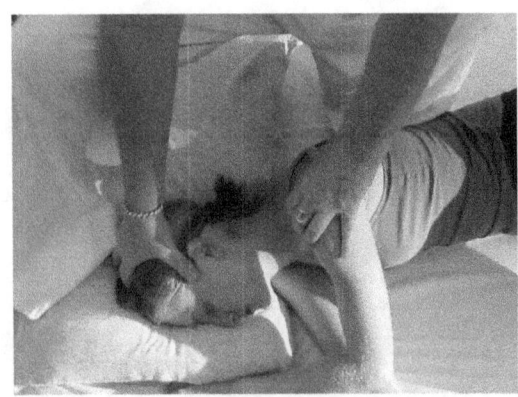
Thumb Circle Around The Ear

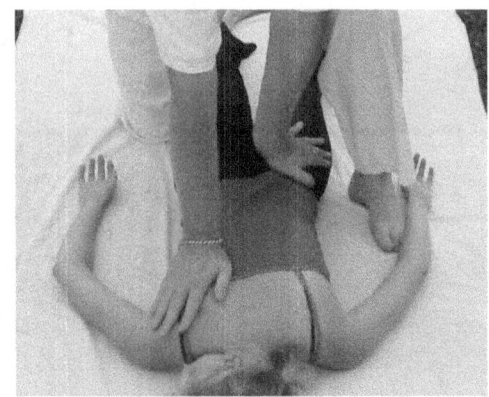
Palm Stretch Back

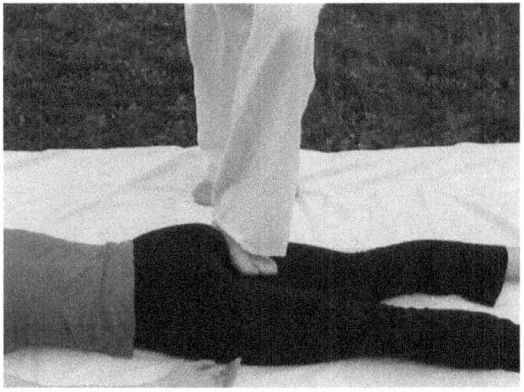

Walk on the upper leg

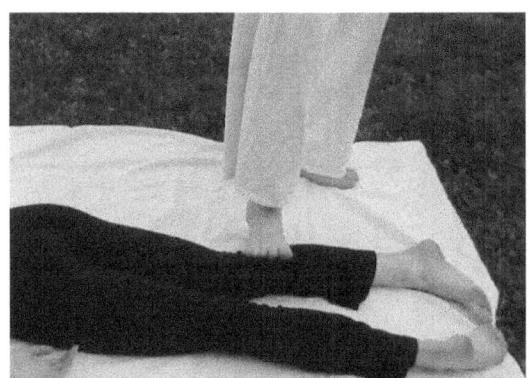

Walk on the lower leg

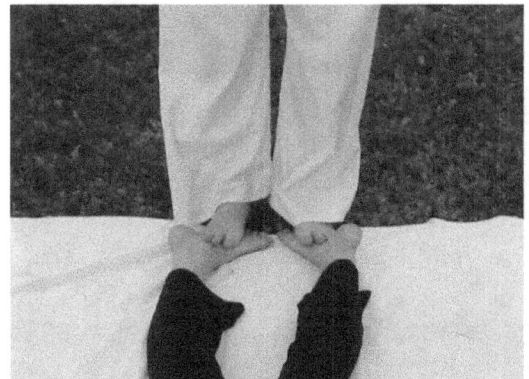

Walk on the feet

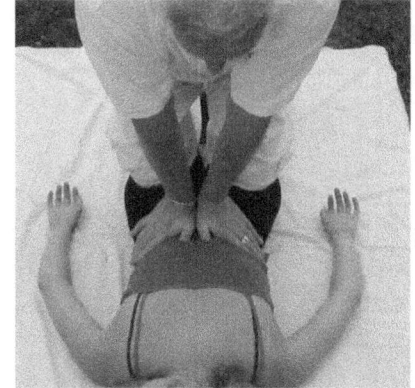

Prone Torso/ Palm Walk

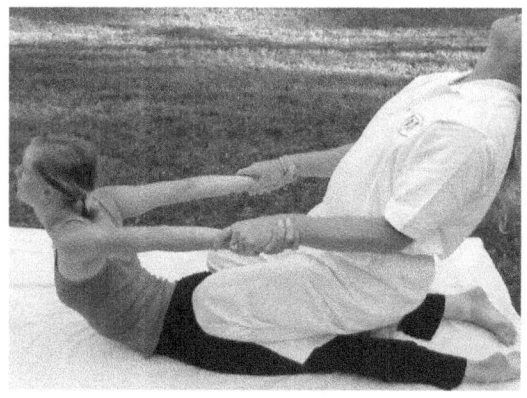

Cobra

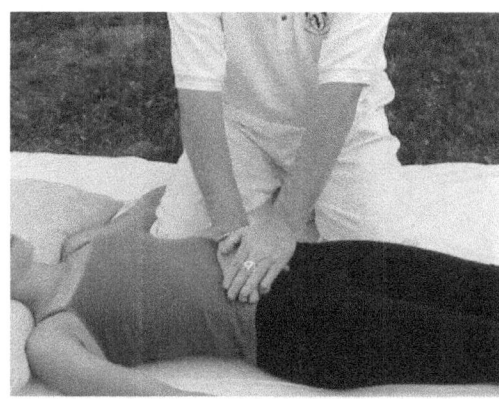

Abdominal Rotations

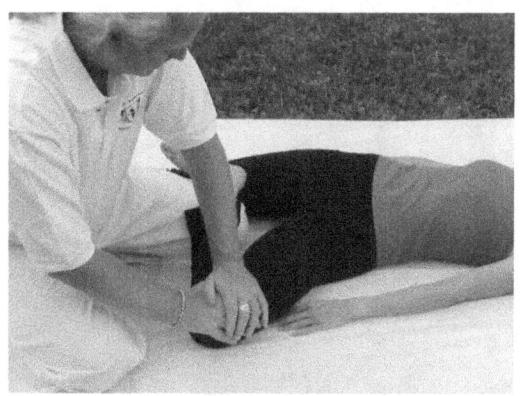

Knee Press

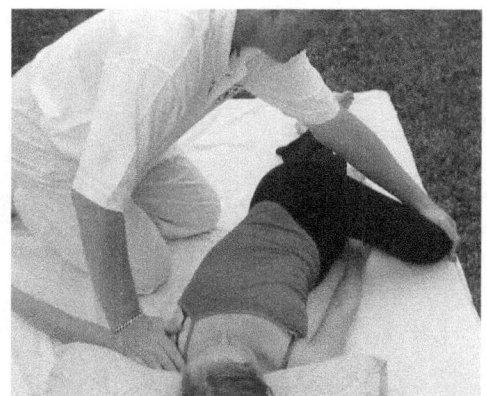

Spinal Rotation

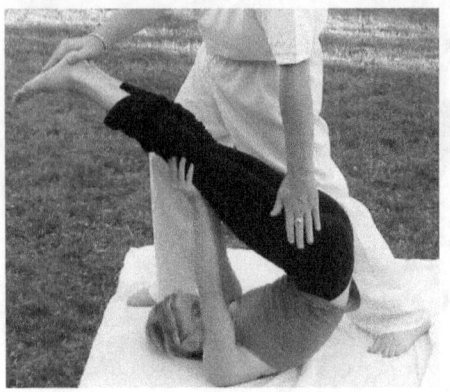

Supported Shoulder Stand

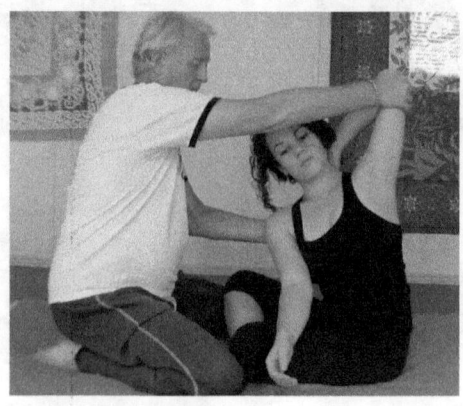

Push the opposite shoulder: Optional

Cross Leg Pull Up

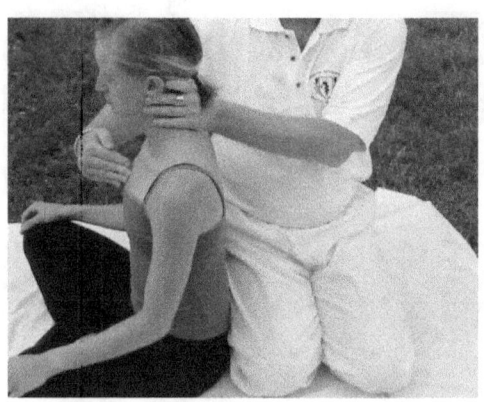

Whale- Beginning position

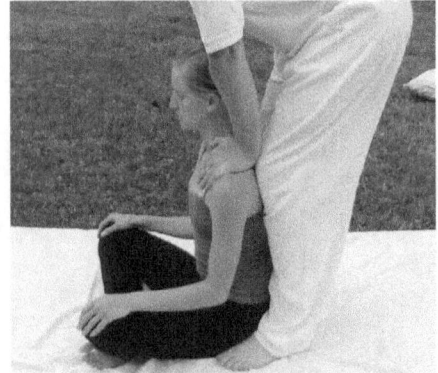

Shoulder Press

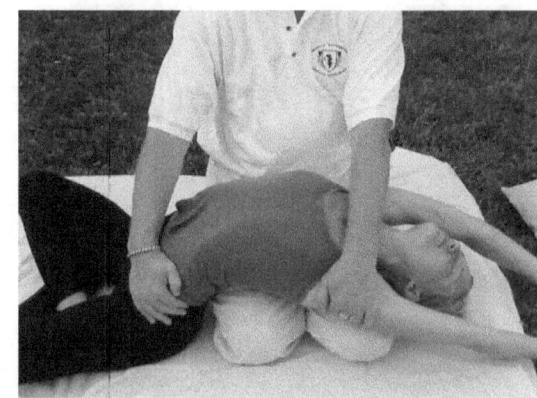

Whale- Ending position

Twist and pull wrist

Forward Bend- Start Position

Forward Bend- Final Position

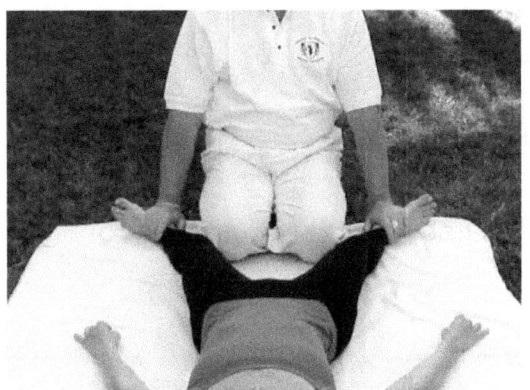

Return to the feet/ Warm-up

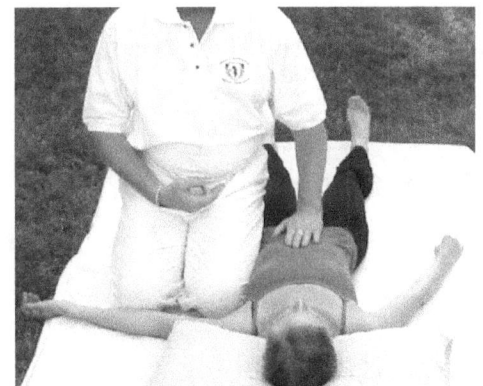

Puja- Finnish

SomaVeda Integrated Traditional Therapies®

We offer training from beginner to Master!

Current NAIC program offerings in the US:
1) Certified SomaVeda® Thai Yoga Practitioner: CTP1 (A 164 CE hour residential training)
2) Certified Ayurveda Wellness Counselor: CTP2 (A 200 CE hour residential training)
3) Certified Ayurveda Health Consultant: CTP3 (A 200 CE hour residential training)
4) Certified SomaVeda® Thai Yoga Teacher: TCP1 (An 1008 CE hour residential training)
5) Doctor of Sacred Natural Medicine Program (DSNM/ ND)(Naturopathic Board Eligibility Course) (A 2595 hour certification program qualifying graduates to sit for the ANCB Naturopathic National Boards. Includes both in-class residential programs and distance learning modules)
6) Doctor of Sacred Traditional and Indigenous Medicine (D.S.T.I.M.) Fast Track "BareBones" Degree in eight to twelve months!
7) Doctor of Integrative Immunity (D.S.I.I.) "BareBones" Degree in twelve to 18 months!

For details on any of the above programs and certification courses, ask your instructor or visit our school website at https://thaiyogacenter.com

SomaVeda® Continuing Education and Practice Building Courses:

https://LearnThaiYoga.Teachable.com

Thai Yoga, Thai Massage Books, DVD, Home Study Courses, Genuine Thai Yoga Mats:

https://BeardedMedia.Com

SomaVeda® Thai Yoga and Thai Massage Products: T-Shirts, Clothing, Posters, Gifts: Official Logo Thai Yoga Center School Uniforms: https://BeardedMedia.Com

Let's connect:
INSTAGRAM: @thaiyogacenter https://www.instagram.com/thaiyogacenter/

FACEBOOK: https://www.facebook.com/anthony.james.733076/ Thai Yoga Center: https://thaiyogacenter.com
American College of Natural Medicine
Learn Thai Yoga Online!
Native American Indigenous Church Tribal Organization

Thai Yoga Stuff! BeardedMedia.com

Official Logo and Image T-shirts and miscellaneous products for office and home.
Hundreds of NAIC, SomaVeda, ACNM, Thai Yoga items and designs!

Logo's, Thai and Spiritual Art goods, and high energy products. Find official cards, posters, banners, and art for your office or home… Great gift idea

Review at home or anytime! Order your SomaVeda® Thai Yoga "Ultimate Thai Massage Video: Basic Mat Techniques " video. It is the same SomaVeda® Thai Yoga Fundamentals of Thai Yoga: Level One Mat that you learned in this class, demonstrated by GM, Ajahn, Dr. Anthony B. James!

$29.95